PRAISE FOR REWRITING FATHERS

"As the father of two young boys one of my life goals is to help them develop a genuine relationship with Jesus Christ. I want to teach them everything I know about the Lord, His Word, and His ways. I love that this book offers an opportunity to leave my deepest thoughts about the Lord in writing for my boys to keep with them when I'm gone. I am so excited about what the Lord is doing through this ministry tool!"

Jared Greer
Father, President of Overcoming Obstacles Ministries, &
Three Time Competitor on American Ninja Warrior
Grandview, TX

"Any person who studies family dynamics understands the powerful importance of the father. An active and present dad who models and teaches a life of submission to King Jesus is sure to bring health and security, as well as proactive spirituality, to the home. Fathers must become intentional in their role as dad to ensure their children have a better understanding of the Heavenly Abba.

Rewriting F.A.T.H.E.R.S. is one of the most unique resources I have seen in a long time. The book is laser-focused on teaching men how to lead their families towards Christ. Every church should prioritize their budget to be able to provide this resource to every dad. Do you want to influence the future for King Jesus? Reach the father."

Richard Ross, Ph.D.
Father, Professor of Student Ministry at Southwestern Seminary
Fort Worth, TX

"As I speak to young people around the world, I often encounter individuals who have lost hope and direction. We should not be surprised that our kids do not have a tenable worldview when we have not 'trained them up' as we are admonished to do.

With Rewriting Fathers, Brandon and Preston have written a compelling book to challenge men to take up their proper role as leaders in the parenting process. This excellent book needs to be read by every man that recognizes he has been placed by God to be the voice of truth to his children in a society that preaches compromise."

Jeff Neal
Father, Former NFL Player, Speaker, Author, & Pastor
Shady Shores, TX

"This is a book every father should read. It gives great spiritual advice and direction of how to be the father your kids deserve, as well as some simple steps on how to apply this to your daily lives. The "leaving a legacy" concept is brilliant and something I'm going to get started on today! This can be passed on generation to generation and give you insight into your fathers life and his feelings you may have never known."

Ron "H20" Waterman
Father, Former UFC & WWE Wrestler, Speaker, & Author
Denver, CO

"I've always felt like people want 'practical' advice and I have styled my own teaching meet that need. Rewriting Fathers gives good, practical advice to Dads."

Dr. David Smith
Father, Senior Pastor of Gracepointe Church
Denton, TX

"Studies show that if a father comes to Christ there is a 96% chance they will lead their family to Jesus as well. If this is true then pastors and churches must prioritize reaching men with the Gospel. Rewriting F.A.T.H.E.R.S. is a practical and easy to use resource for dads that teach men how to parent intentionally.

This is also a great tool for churches to use in small groups or men's accountability groups. However you choose to implement this in your church, get a copy for every man in your congregation. It will be worth the investment."

Russell Allen
Father, Senior Pastor of Woodlawn Baptist Church
Austin, TX

"It's not often that men with excessive youth can provide a ready tool for fathers to use to discharge the awesome responsibility of parenthood, but Preston and Brandon have done it. Succinct, scriptural, and satisfying. I enthusiastically recommend Rewriting Fathers to every church desiring to impact the future of our fatherless society."

E. Dale Hill
Father, President of Encore Church Resources, & Director of Missions at Burnet Llano Baptist Association
Lago Vista, TX

"Having a resource to help fathers start embodying biblical manhood is an awesome thing for me and the men in our church. I get so tired of the world dictating what it means to be a man. It's refreshing to finally have a understandable and repeatable resource that helps Fathers grasp biblical manhood. As a father I can't wait to use this resource when tucking my kids in at night to be a catechism of sorts on what it means to be a man and father. It will teach my children what to expect from me; my son what he must be and my daughter what 'he' must be to be her husband."

Dr. Todd Gray
Father, Former USAF Captain, & Pastor of Tabernacle Church
Ennis, TX

"My first son was born in 1999. This was a shock because when I first got married I was told I couldn't have kids. I was told this by my Mother In-Law and turns out she was very wrong. Anyway, I now have 5 tax deductions. They are all boys so our house smells like if a foot could pass gas. Being a father is my favorite job, but its a tough job. I could've really used this book when I first started. I've read it twice through now because our wi-fi is very bad and I can't get Netflix to load while 5 boys play Fortnite. This book is the perfect guide for fathers on how to raise your children through life's twists and turns and keep them on the right path. It also tells a story about me changing a flat tire so that alone should make it a best seller!"

Bob Smiley
Father, Comedian
The Woodlands, TX

"This is a great book for dads of all ages. Not only is it simple to read and understand, but any father, young or old, can read through it and digest the content quickly. Even older dads will find plenty of useful information to apply in their own families, no matter their stage of life. Great job!"

Bryce Ulrich
Father, Executive Pastor of Mississippi Avenue Baptist Church
Aurora, CO

"As a mother of three, I'm looking forward to seeing Rewriting Fathers inspire and cultivate dads everywhere. The impact will be immeasurable to fathers, families, and their children for generations to come. It is God-centered and strong, yet simple. It is sure to help fathers leave a lasting legacy."

Andrea Gibson
Mother, Director of Communications at Northview Baptist Church
Lewisville, TX

"In Rewriting FATHERS the message is strong, clear, and intentional...capturing the essence of what it means to be a father and relating it to real-life experiences. The Christian principles in this book are authentic, powerful and provide a guide for understanding the important role God intended for fathers.

At a time when society needs men to step up and embrace their biblical role to lead the family and engage in the world around them, this book serves as a valuable tool to help men become better husbands and fathers, while simultaneously enabling them to leave a lasting legacy for their own children."

Dr. Jeremy Glenn
Father, Superintendent of Granbury ISD
Granbury, TX

"Rewriting Fathers will challenge, inspire, and encourage you as a Father. It will help prepare you to leave a legacy with you children that will bless them greatly."

Norman Flowers
Father, Missions & Discipleship Pastor
Marble Falls, TX

"Preston & Brandon have done a great job of not only defining what a good father looks like, but also giving a great blueprint to teach your sons how to become a great father. Use this guide with your sons to teach them how to become a good father or use it with your daughters to teach them what to look for in a good husband. Every father will benefit from this great resource."

Wayne Slay
Father, Groups Pastor of Avenue Church
Waxahachie, TX

"I have spent the last few years mentoring and counseling couples in marriage to better strengthen the family and I can tell you from experience that there are few resources today specifically geared towards helping men know how to be strong, Godly fathers and husbands. There are even fewer resources that are actually practical, applicable, and ready to use straight off the shelf.

Rewriting Fathers is one of the best new resources that dads can use. Every father needs to get his hands on this book."

Billy Beacham
Father, See You At The Pole National Coordinator and President of Student Discipleship Ministries

"Preston and Brandon Cave in their book Rewriting Fathers, have given us an excellent first step into spiritually functional fatherhood.

Using this simple acronym F.A.T.H.E.R.S. these brothers share timeless wisdom for first time dads as well as seasoned grandfathers. They remind us of what is important rather than what feels urgent."

Dr. Mark Forrest
Father, Senior Pastor at Lakeside Baptist Church
Granbury, TX

Rewriting FATHERS

An easy to remember approach to fatherhood with a legacy journal to pass on to your children.

Co-written by
BRANDON CAVE & PRESTON CAVE

Book Credits:
First revisions by Sarah & Brit Cave
Edited by Jes Finton
Sketches throughout by Brit Cave
Cover & Inside Graphics by Brandon Cave

ISBN: 978-1-7330633-0-2
@ Copyright 2019, Rewriting Fathers, Brandon Cave & Preston Cave

This book is dedicated to, and is a product of, our late father, Bobby Cave. He led us to find Jesus, challenged us to dig deeper, and pushed us to become more than we could ever see in ourselves.

We love you, Dad. Thanks for the legacy.

Thank you also to our wives, Brit & Sarah, who make us better men and better fathers, and to our children, who inspire us to make the world a better place.

-Brandon & Preston

TABLE OF CONTENTS

FOREWORD

CHAPTER 1 - A FATHER'S PURPOSE   1

CHAPTER 2 - F: FATHERS ARE FAITHFUL   5

CHAPTER 3 - A: FATHERS ARE AVAILABLE   13

CHAPTER 4 - T: FATHERS ARE TEACHABLE   17

CHAPTER 5 - H: FATHERS HELP & HEAL   23

CHAPTER 6 - E: FATHERS ENCOURAGE & EQUIP   27

CHAPTER 7 - R: FATHERS RAISE & REDIRECT   31

CHAPTER 8 - S: FATHERS SERVE & SHARE   35

CHAPTER 9 - THE LEGACY JOURNAL   41

JOURNAL PROMPTS   44

THE GREAT EXCHANGE   122

TEACHING THESE PRINCIPLES TO YOUR KIDS   124

FOREWORD

Inside out. These two words are so powerful that if this principle were put into practice it could change the world. What do I mean by these two words? Consider the Geode. Geodes are spherical rock structures with an internal cavity lined with mineral materials. They have a rough and rocky exterior that is more resistant to weathering than the surrounding bedrock, which allows the minerals inside to be protected and perfectly preserved for years. The exterior is anticlimactic, but once cracked open the treasure inside is astonishing. Some Geodes even sell in decor shops for thousands of dollars!

Imagine how many of these beautiful rocks have been overlooked throughout the centuries by explorers looking for "real" treasures. Imagine the surprise of the people who first discovered how incredible a piece of art these commonplace stones could produce. Think about it for a moment. Something that looks so bland on the outside could contain such majesty and honor on the inside. I could think of no better illustration to communicate the impact and influence that is contained within the average father.

"Inside out" is my way of challenging us, as dads, to live the life we were created to live. No matter what our external features may be, we all have treasure, dignity and a legacy living within us. It must be remembered that you and I were created in the image of God, which means we are the Imago Dei (Image of God). This means we are called to reflect the One we were created to imitate. God is a good Father and we are called to be as well. No matter our outer exterior, our inner being is the Imago Dei. Because of this, we must choose each day to live from the inside out.

However, many men today fear revealing what is on the inside due to our own insecurities and quite often from wounds left by absent or abusive fathers. This leads to the belief that we have nothing on the inside worth displaying. Men will focus on the exterior to hide what we think we know about the interior. The sad reality is most men haven't allowed themselves to be cracked open enough to discover the hidden splendor of their hearts. If only we would be authentic with ourselves we would become more aware of the Imago Dei living within us. Then, the cycle of neglect or abuse would cease. Then a new and exciting future might be birthed as fathers lived and parented from the inside out.

More young men and women would learn to be transparent as they watch their father live the Imago Dei in front of them. Dads would begin to see the potential in their kids instead of the immediate reality. Children and teenagers would learn to dream a better future as they learn to see the Imago Dei within themselves, as well as those around them. The potential is endless if inside out living becomes the norm. Imagine the future dividends we would have if fathers decided to live this way.

As an athlete, motivational speaker, and founder of the Two Words Character Development Curriculum I have traveled the globe challenging young people to live the inside out principle. I have seen many embrace this challenge. But now it is time for a new generation to step up and lead. Fathers are the most influential people in the family and it is time for us to lead our families well. I have known Brandon and Preston as colaborers in ministry and as friends for many years and I absolutely love what they have done with this resource. You are holding one of the most powerful tools in helping us, as fathers, know how to live that inside out principle in front of our wife and children. Don't waste this opportunity to be inspired and equipped by them as they challenge us all to rewrite the future of a fatherless society. It is time to become men who fight for the family, fight for purity, fight for integrity, and fight for authenticity. It is time for us to be cracked open in order to reveal the honor, majesty & legacy within us. It is time for us to help our families discover the Imago Dei living within them as well. It is time for us as F.A.T.H.E.R.S. to truly live inside out.

Stephen Mackey
Father, Speaker, & Founder of 2Words Character Development
www.2words.tv - www.mackeyspeaks.com

CHAPTER 1:
A FATHER'S PURPOSE

Rewriting
FATHERS

Chapter 1: A Father's Purpose

Jim Gaffigan once joked, "But truly, women are amazing. Think about it this way: a woman can grow a baby inside her body. Then a woman can deliver the baby through her body. Then, by some miracle, a woman can feed a baby with her body. When you compare that to the male's contribution to life, it's kind of embarrassing, really."[1] While this is a rather humorous (and somewhat accurate) observation, it really only addresses conception, birth, and infancy.

The real truth about the effects of fathers on life is that we are extremely important to the physical, emotional, mental, and spiritual development of our sons and daughters. In fact, studies consistently show that children with active and present fathers in their lives are likely to be happier and do better in school, and are less likely to engage in substance abuse, be arrested, or struggle with emotional insecurity.

Research has also shown that children experience an increase in negative emotions and behaviors when their father is absent (physically or emotionally), including greater sadness, withdrawal and anxiety, increased aggression, impulsivity and hyperactivity.[2]

"Train up a child in the way he should go; even when he is old he will not depart from it." says Proverbs 22:6 (ESV). But what if you simply don't know how?

As you read this, you probably desire to be a positive role model in the life of your family. The challenge isn't the lack of desire to be a good dad. The challenge is that most of us have no idea how to be a good father. Many men today grew up in a fatherless home, or one with a father who was physically present but emotionally absent. Consequently, men who become fathers develop a hidden insecurity rooted in the fear of being a failure at raising children, yet the male pride usually keeps us from asking for help.

What if there was a simple litmus test to help us know if we were fathering well? What if we could also use that litmus test as a customizable father/child curriculum to teach our children what it means to be a good father? If we have a son, we could use the outline to show him how to be a father when he gets married and has kids. If we are raising a daughter, we can use the same framework to help her understand what type of man her future husband should be.

Rewriting Fathers is our way of equipping fathers with a strategy for raising their children while also providing future fathers with a job description of what a father IS and what a father DOES. The following pages will be divided into two parts. Part #1 addresses what a father IS. Part #2 looks at what a father DOES. Before we begin, let me give you the general outline, which happens to be an acronym of the word F.A.T.H.E.R.S.

What a Father IS:

    F - Faithful

    A - Available

    T - Teachable

What a Father DOES:

    H - Helps and Heals

    E - Encourages and Equips

    R - Raises and Redirects

    S - Serves and Shares

This is what a father IS and what a father DOES. Interested in learning how to be a better father? If so, then read on!

A father is neither an anchor to hold us back nor a sail to take us there, but a guiding light whose love shows us the way.

WHAT A FATHER IS

CHAPTER 2:
FATHERS ARE
FAITHFUL

Rewriting
FATHERS

Chapter 2: Fathers Are Faithful

The word faithful can be defined as loyal, constant, and steadfast. It doesn't sound all that sexy, but it is one of the most powerful attributes a father can possess. To be the father God has called us to be, we must embrace, and not neglect, this attribute. But what does it mean to be faithful? We will look at four areas in which a father is called to be faithful and then will give a few practical steps towards living a life of faithfulness.

Faithful to our God
The first place in which we should be faithful is with God. A father is always faithful to God. What does it mean to have a faithful spirit towards God? Let me answer this question by sharing a story.

Many years ago I was working for an evangelistic ministry traveling around the country serving churches of all shapes and sizes. I was making a whopping $18,000 a year doing full-time ministry. We were always faithful to tithe though. I remember one day I was sitting on my couch in our single-wide trailer house when God asked me to give more money that month for my tithe. I was thinking, "God, I wasn't even talking to you! I was just watching TV. What do you mean 'give more this month?' We are barely making it as it is." But I knew it was Him talking.

By the way, how can you tell if it is God and not you talking? A good test is to ask these questions about what you feel God has said to you:

    1. Does this violate any teaching in the Bible?
    2. Would Satan tell me to do this?
    3. Would I tell myself to do this?
    4. Would doing this help build the kingdom of God?

What God asked me to do that day didn't violate Scripture. I knew Satan wouldn't tell me to give more money to the church. I KNEW I wouldn't tell myself to give more to the church, since we didn't have any more to give. And I knew it would, indeed, help build the kingdom of God. But I told God he would have to convince my wife. I thought that would surely put an end to this discussion.

When my wife got home, I said, "Honey, I think God wants us to give more in our tithe this month. What do you think?" She looked at me and said without hesitation, "If that's what you think God wants us to do, then let's do it." Side note: this is the type of spouse you want to marry, and that's the type of spouse you want to be. That next Sunday, I wrote a check out for more than we usually gave.

I was driving to the city later that Sunday for an event and I was feeling pretty good about myself. Without warning, the next thing I knew, the car in front of me locked up their brakes in the middle of a busy street. I had nowhere to go but up their tail pipe. I rear-ended them! I immediately thought, "God! What are you doing? I gave you more money today. You were supposed to bless me." See how easy it is to blame God? And how easy it is to expect a quick return on our investments? The truth is, the wreck wasn't God's fault and He was never obligated to bless me because of my obedience. But he chose to bless me nonetheless.

The next week I received a rental car from my insurance company. They totaled out my cheap little car and gave me more than what I owed on it. We then were able to find a vehicle that only had 1,500 miles on it, although it was a few years old. It was the same price per month as what we were originally paying on the junk car.

I was floating on cloud nine. I then received a call from my ministry office. It was the president of our ministry, and he informed me that they had decided to give me a raise. I was obviously excited. I asked how much. He said, "How about a $7,000 raise?"

Listen. God already had plans to bless my family before he even asked me to give a little more one month. When he asks us to do something that doesn't seem "doable" we should know that God is in the business of doing the "undoable." We should trust Him.

To be faithful to God means being obedient to Him even when it doesn't make any sense. Years ago, Eugene Peterson wrote a book called *A Long Obedience in the Same Direction*. That title captures fully the thought of what it means to be faithful to God.

Be faithful to our God.

Faithful to our Family
The second place in which we should be faithful is with our family. A father is always faithful to his family. Family is a place where life

happens more freely. Family is where we can be "ourselves" all the time. Did you realize that parents have about 3,000 hours per year with their children? Compare this to the 40-50 hours per year the church has with the average student. Which institution do you think has the greatest potential for influence? For better or worse, the family has so much more potential impact. So, let's regularly find ways to be faithful to our family.

Hopefully, you have an open relationship and an open line of communication with your family. This is an essential component to being faithful to our family. Bible study is so much better with the family in the living room. Scripture is more potent when read with your spouse in the bedroom. Spiritual conversations are so much deeper in the realm of a healthy relationship with family members.

As fathers, we have the potential to be the most significant influence on our kids and spouse. But we must teach them by our words and by our actions what faithfulness is. Faithfulness to our family means being more committed to them than to our career. It means honoring and prioritizing them more than even ourselves. Jesus once said that we should love our neighbor as ourselves (Matthew 22:39). We must look at our family as our neighbor, too. We should love them and treat them the way we want them to love and treat us. Also, we should ask this fundamental question:

How is my relationship with my wife and kids going to reveal the glory of God in them and reveal the glory of God in me?

Be faithful to our family.

Faithful to our Church
The third place in which we should be faithful is with our church. A father is always faithful to his church. The church is a place where we connect with Jesus through his people. This is a place where we can learn how to forgive others, confess our struggles, collaborate together, worship, and serve. The church is the second institution God established to fulfill his great commission to reach the world with the good news of Jesus, and it is the Bride of Christ.

What does it mean to be faithful to the church? It means being more committed to Jesus' Bride than to our desires. It means honoring and prioritizing her more than even ourselves. Again, Jesus tells us to love our neighbor as ourselves. We must look at our church as our neighbor, too. We should love her and treat her the way we want others to love and treat our family.

Every time I see someone on the side of a road changing a flat tire I look to see if it is a man or a woman. If it is a man, I usually keep driving because I know they either already know how to change a tire, or they need to learn how to change a tire. But, if it is a woman, I always stop to help. I stop because I would want someone to stop to help my wife if she were in that predicament.

I remember a day when my wife was in that predicament. She called me and asked if I could come help her. There was one problem: I was over an hour away from her. She was stranded on the side of a busy highway and I was a long way in coming to her rescue.

While I was still on the phone with her, I heard an unexpectedly familiar voice in the background. It was Bob Smiley! He is a popular Christian comedian and he just happened to see her on the side of the road. He stopped and helped her change the tire. I was so grateful for the help, and I felt like my wife was honored and protected. If I felt this way towards a person being faithful to my bride how much more does God feel towards a person being faithful to His bride?

Being faithful to our church means always speaking positively about the members and the leadership. It means being regular attendees and not just CEO Christians (Christmas and Easter Only). It means being financially faithful to the ministry of the church. We don't withhold finances from our family, so don't withhold finances from God's family. Lastly, when thinking about what it means to be faithful to the church, we should ask this fundamental question:

How is my relationship with my church going to reveal the glory of God in her and reveal the glory of God in me?

Be faithful to our church.

Faithful to our Work
The fourth place in which we should be faithful is with our work. A father is always faithful to his work. This does not mean we shouldn't try to progress in our career, or that we should turn down a better job when the opportunity makes itself available to us. What it means is we should be faithful to our current employer,

and to complete the job we have to the best of our ability.

A faithful worker is the type employers look to promote. Some men scratch their heads in confusion wondering why they get overlooked for every promotion. Sometimes the variables are outside of our control. However, unfortunately many times it is because we haven't been as faithful to our company as we could be.

Have you ever said anything negative about your work or employer? Do you come in with a positive attitude or a toxic demeanor? Are you always showing up on time, or better yet, early? Are you willing to stay a few minutes late to get the job done correctly?

I remember walking into a fast food restaurant months ago and I was greeted by a young man who seemed to be a good worker. He was friendly and engaging as he took my order. Everything was great until the end of the visit. During the final payment process, his boss came out from the back and asked him to do something, which didn't sound like a very big task. After the boss left, the young man leaned over and whispered something very vulgar and negative about his boss. I was shocked by his audacity to say that to anyone, much less a customer. At that moment I knew this guy wouldn't be promoted in this company, and he probably wouldn't be there long either.

You might be thinking, "Yeah, but it is an entry-level fast food position. He probably doesn't want to be there long anyway." You might be right, but there is a way to be promoted, and there is a way of getting fired. As long as he is unfaithful to his current position and current boss, he will never move past his current level of employment. A good father understands the need to take care of his family monetarily; he will be faithful to his work to meet those needs.

Some men today bounce from job to job for no reason other than they become bored or discontent with their work. There may be a time to leave your position, but if at all possible, try to tough it out until you have another job lined up. This will help you not have a gap in your paycheck, which will ensure care for your family. Don't let your pride, anger, or ambitions get in the way of the needs of your family. The only time you should leave a position quickly is if the reason for leaving falls under the M.E.L.T. principle.

What is the M.E.L.T. Principle? M.E.L.T. stands for:

M - Moral
E - Ethical
L - Legal
T - Theological

If an issue violates one of these four categories, then you might consider terminating your current employment. For example, is the reason you want to leave because the company, or employer, is breaking the law? Or maybe there is something morally wrong with the environment? Perhaps, the ethics of the company are not honoring God. Whatever the reason may be, I still advise trying to line up a new job BEFORE leaving the current position. If it is at all possible, we should be faithful to our work and regard it, not only as a provision for our family but also as worship to our God.

A father is FAITHFUL to his God, his family, his church, and his work.

Bible Study Option
1. Read and discuss: Luke 19:12-25
2. What can we learn about being faithful in this parable?
3. How does this principle of being faithful apply to our family? To our church?
4. What is one thing you will do this week to display faithfulness to your family?
5. How will you teach this principle to your children this week?
6. Can I hold you accountable to do this?

Every father should remember that one day, his kids will follow his example, not just his advice.

WHAT A FATHER IS

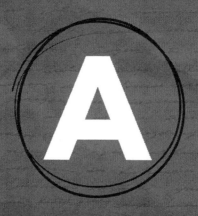

CHAPTER 3:
FATHERS ARE
AVAILABLE

Rewriting
FATHERS

Chapter 3: Fathers Are Available

The next word in the acronym is the word AVAILABLE. What does it mean to be available? It means that time is involved. How do you spell love? "T-I-M-E" because love takes TIME. So, to be a father that leaves a positive legacy, we are going to have to put in the time.

Available to our God
The first place in which we should be available is with God. A father is always available to God. What does it mean to be available to God? Well, if we will focus on being faithful to God, then being available to Him will come more naturally. Faithfulness to God tends to cultivate availability to Him.

When I was in middle school, I played on the school football team. I was, and still am, a small person. Needless to say, I was not a starting player. Nevertheless, I was available to the team and I always showed up and practiced hard. My coach would always tell us that if we wanted to play in the game, then we would need to stand close to him in between plays. He would need to send in a sub from time-to-time to get the next play to our quarterback. He often told us, "If you really want to play, then make eye contact with me when I start to look around."

I would often stand next to him for several plays watching and waiting for the opportunity to catch his eye. When he would begin to look around, I would stare directly at his eyes until he made eye contact with me. Then he would put me in the game. This is a perfect picture of what it means to be available to God. Wait on the Lord and catch His eye when he looks for someone to put in the game.

Be available to our God.

Available to our Family
The second place in which we should be available is with our family. A father is always available to his family. A story is told of a father and a son. The father was very busy but had promised his son that he would take him on a fishing trip. Finally, the day arrived when the dad was able to take an afternoon off from work, and he decided to fulfill his promise to his son. They spent several hours together in a small flat-bottom boat on a frog-infested pond. After a long time with no success in catching anything, the dad decided it was time to call it quits. Later that night the dad wrote in his journal, "Went fishing with little Johnny. We didn't talk, and we didn't catch a single fish. Total waste of time!" At the

same moment, little Johnny wrote in his journal, "My dad took me fishing... BEST DAY EVER!"

You see, to our children, it isn't the success or the failure of an event. It is the EVENT itself. Being available to our wife and kids will be easier than we think. We just need to set aside our laptops and cell phones for a significant amount of time and simply look them in the eyes. If our kids are young, then roll around with them on the carpet. If they are older, then play video games or watch a movie together. Take them out for ice cream or bowling. Anything will do as long as it is with you.

Sometimes teenagers don't seem to want to spend time with us, but deep down they just want us to fight for their time. They want to be pursued. So pursue them! Fight for the family and be committed to "Going Analog" from time to time. What do I mean by "Going Analog" though? My family has instituted a few times each week where we "go analog" by putting away all electronic devices and sitting together as we read a REAL book or play a REAL board game together. These are special times where we, as fathers, can be present and AVAILABLE to our families.

Be available to our family.

Available to our Church
The third place in which we should be available is with our church. A father is always available to his church. When we schedule our week, month, or year, we should always budget time for the church first. Giving the church the first priority in our schedule shows God that we are willing to be available to His bride in our lives. Are you always available to serve His bride weekly, or are you more of a leech on the bride? Do you ever consider going on a mission trip sometime during the year? Have you ever asked God if there was anything He wanted you to do for the church? If not, then maybe you need to reconsider whether you are actually being available to your church. We need the body of Christ, and the body of Christ needs us.

Be available to our Church.

Available to our Work
The fourth place in which we should be available is with our work. A father is always available to his work. Notice that work comes after God, Family, and Church. Being available to our work does not mean we neglect our relationship with God, our family, or our church. Too many men prioritize work over everything else. If we are not careful, we will begin to find our identity in what we DO rather than who we ARE. You and I are children of God BEFORE

anything else. And we are fathers to our families BEFORE we are workers for our careers. This is important to get our priorities in proper order.

There will be times when work demands our time and undivided attention. But it is our job, as fathers, to have a healthy balance between work and family. When I say, "we should be available to our work," what I DON'T mean is we should neglect our family due to our work. I mean we should not be lazy with work, and we should give our job 100% of our effort when we are working. The healthiest fathers I have encountered are the dads that know when to work and when to stop working. There is a time to be in the office, and there is a time to be at home. When we are at the office, we should be available to our work. When we are at home, we need to give our undivided attention to our family. Lance Witt says in his book, *High Impact Teams*, that God designed life not to be lived in balance, but in rhythm.[3] The rhythm looks like this:

Work, then REST. Produce, then RESTORE. Go hard, then STOP. Exert energy, then REPLENISH energy. Empty your bucket, then FILL your bucket. If we can figure out how to live in this God-ordained rhythm then we will not neglect our family while still being available to our work.

A father is AVAILABLE to his God, his family, his church, and his work.

Bible Study Option
1. Read and discuss: Matthew 4:18-22
2. How did the early disciples give us an example of being available?
3. Do you think it was hard for them to leave everything they had to be available to Jesus?
4. Read and discuss: Matthew 19:16-22
5. Why did the rich young ruler walk away sad?
6. What are the significant differences between the story of the disciples and the story of the rich young ruler?
7. What are you not willing to give up for Jesus right now?
8. Will you consider giving Jesus ALL of your life this week?
9. Can I hold you accountable to do this?

WHAT A FATHER IS

CHAPTER 4:
FATHERS ARE
TEACHABLE

Rewriting
FATHERS

Chapter 4: Fathers Are Teachable

The third word in the acronym is the word TEACHABLE. This is the last word in the "What a Father IS" section. We all know the guy who knows it all. By the way, if you don't know that guy, then chances are you *are* that guy. But we all know people who always think they are right and never seem to be open to correction or critique. These people are rather annoying and could use a good beating from time-to-time. Just kidding... sort of. Anyway, a good father recognizes that noone is perfect and we all lack something. A good father always has a teachable spirit.

Teachable to our God
The first place in which we should be teachable is with God. A father is always teachable to God. How can we learn to be teachable towards God? Being teachable to God means actually putting into practice what we hear.

Let me answer with an illustration: I have seven large pecan trees in my yard. They shed dead branches all the time. What if I walked outside one day and began screaming at the dead branches to produce pecans? Would they be able to do so? No. Why? Because they are no longer connected to the source necessary to receive the proper nutrients to produce pecans. On the flip side, what if I went outside and demanded the healthy trees to stop producing pecans? Would they be able to obey? No. Why not? The only option, for a branch that is connected to a healthy tree, is to produce the fruit of that tree.

Jesus once told his disciples, in order for them to produce fruit, they would need to remain in Him. In other words, Jesus needed them to connect with Him and to stay connected to Him, like a branch is connected to a tree. Like a tree, the system is only effective [in producing fruit] when all the parts work together. The roots absorb the nutrients from the ground and deliver it to the trunk. The trunk stores and distributes those nutrients to the branches. The branches then produce fruit. It's that simple. For us to actually live a life of teachability toward God, we need to stay connected to Jesus. But how do we do this? Let me give you a strategy that might help.

I suggest we make it a habit, and a priority, to connect with Jesus daily, weekly, monthly, and yearly. What do I mean? We call this strategy C4, aptly named after the commonly known plastic explosive C4. When we apply this strategy, our lives can truly become explosive. Here, C4 stands for "Connect Four" and it focuses on us, connecting to Jesus in four unique ways to better ensure we will be teachable to God; daily, weekly, monthly, and yearly.

Daily
The first way we should connect to God is through His word daily. Begin each day with a "verse-of-the-day" or a chapter of the Bible. Find a men's devotional book and read a section each day. Whatever it looks like for you to connect to God daily may be different for each of us. No matter how you do this, it is vital to connect to Him in some way each day.

Weekly
The second way to connect to God is through His people weekly. I know the schedule doesn't always make this easy, but if we prioritize not missing a sporting event maybe we should also prioritize not missing time spent with God through His people. Being teachable to God means being teachable to His bride, the Church.

Think about it this way. If a friend disregarded everything your spouse said because they didn't see value in her, would you have a close relationship with that person? Chances are the answer is "NO!" Why? Because they disrespected your bride and you love your bride more than you love that friend. How much more does Jesus care about His bride than we do our bride? God often speaks to us through His bride, so we better listen up. Remember: what we prioritize, our kids will also prioritize. If church attendance isn't important to us, then it won't be important to our kids.

Monthly
The third way to connect to God is through an accountability partner or a mentor. Think about it. To become men of integrity, we must sit in an apprenticeship-type relationship with older men of integrity. Integrity doesn't happen by accident. It takes work. Be willing to put in the hard work of being teachable through accountable relationships with other men in the church.

Yearly
The fourth way to connect to God is through extracurricular events. An extracurricular event is any activity not part of your church's weekly or monthly schedule. This is the fun part. Look at your calendar throughout the year and plan times for spiritual refreshment. Take your family to a Christian concert. Spend time

with your spouse at a marriage retreat. Go to a special event with your small group and connect to Jesus. Everybody needs events throughout the year to be a spiritual "shot in the arm" so they will refocus on the main thing.

If you need help implementing the C4 strategy, you can grab a C4 Journal at: www.rewritingfathers.com

Be teachable to our God.

Teachable to our Family
The second place in which we should be teachable is with our family. A father is always teachable to his family. Does this mean we have to check our brains at the door or live in total submission to whatever our family decides? Of course not. Fathers are the spiritual leaders of the home. But this does not mean we know more than everybody else in our family. There are times I submit to the wisdom of my wife because she is more knowledgeable at certain things than I am.

Paul mentions something very interesting in Ephesians chapter five. As men, we tend to enjoy the verse that commands wives to submit to their husbands, as to the Lord. *"For the husband is the head of the wife even as Christ is the head of the church,"* (Ephesians 5:23) But many men often miss the verse immediately before this verse. Ephesians 5:21 actually says, "Submitting to one another out of reverence for Christ." Wait a second! I thought my job as the husband was to lead my wife and kids? Well, of course that is our job, but that job doesn't mean we don't, at times, submit to our wife.

What does it mean to submit to another person? It doesn't mean following blindly. It means being teachable to others by listening to and regarding their thoughts and feelings as something worth considering. It also means we should always strive to be a student of our family. We should listen to understand and attempt to discover what makes each member of our family tick.

Stop thinking of this as a "family" for a moment. Think of your "family unit" as an organization with employees. Any leader worth his salt will be a student of people and will learn from as many individuals in that organization as possible to better lead the company. Does the leader lose any authority or value because he submits to those under his leadership? No. In fact, submitting to others from time-to-time will actually make him a better leader. If this is true in a business setting, how much more true is it in a family unit? Fathers may be the spiritual leader of the home, but we need to always remain teachable to the different members of our family so we can effectively lead them well.

Be teachable to our family.

Teachable to our Church
The third place in which we should be teachable is with our church. A father is always teachable to his church. The church is the second institution God established for discipleship to take place. This means if we want to be taught, we must sit under the authority of a spiritual leader whom God has placed over us. We men don't usually like to sit under the authority of anyone. However, learning to hear from God through other people will help us hear His voice more clearly.

God speaks to us in three significant ways. He speaks through His word. He speaks through prayer. He speaks through His people. If this is true, then we shouldn't neglect to gather with His people and to sit under the spiritual authority of a pastor who has been called by God and trained to teach God's word. Pastors are one of God's instruments for teaching His people. If we really want to be teachable, we must be teachable to our church as well.

Be teachable to our church.

Teachable to our Work
The fourth place in which we should be teachable is with our work. A father is always teachable to his work. What does it mean to be teachable to our work? It means being lifelong learners. Depending on your career you might need to receive higher education and get a degree; but, not every job or position will require this. However, every career or position will require us educating ourselves to be the best we can be while on the job.

A good father will seek opportunities to be trained in his field so he can work with excellence. This is so important for us to do for the sake of our kids. Our children will often develop the same work ethic we display. If we aren't concerned with performing our jobs with excellence, don't be surprised when our children don't perform in school with excellence. We should take ownership of our work and learn as much as we can in our field to grow in our abilities. This not only will open us up to possible promotions in the future, but it will also teach our children to work at everything they do with as much excellence as they can.

There is a lost art in the workplace today. It is called work ethic and lifelong learning. What would your future look like if you developed a habit of being teachable to your boss and your company? It would not only pay dividends to you personally, but it would help you leave a positive legacy to your children by them also living as lifelong learners.

Be teachable to our work.

A father is TEACHABLE to his God, his family, his church, and his work.

Bible Study Option

1. Read and discuss: James 3:13-18
2. What is the difference between knowledge and wisdom?
3. Is it possible to have knowledge without having wisdom? Explain.
4. Even though this passage doesn't use the word "teachable," what can we learn about the importance of remaining teachable?
5. What is one thing you will do this week to be teachable?
6. Can I hold you accountable to do this?

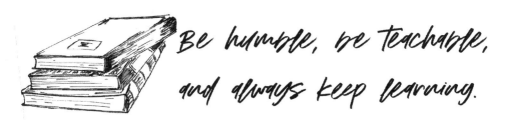

Be humble, be teachable, and always keep learning.

WHAT A FATHER DOES

CHAPTER 5:
HELP AND HEAL

Rewriting
FATHERS

Chapter 5: Fathers Help and Heal

In this section, we will shift from looking at what a father IS to reviewing what a father DOES. We will be focusing strictly on the family. There are certain things every father should do for his family. Obviously, we don't have space to write down everything a father should do, and each family is different. But the following pages communicate the "At Least" principle. The "At Least" principle teaches there are some things every father should at least do. You may not be able to do everything other fathers do, but you can, and should, at least do the following things for your family. Make sense? Let's get started...

The fourth letter in the acronym stands for two words: HELP and HEAL. Let's spend a few moments talking about each word and discuss a few examples of what it looks like to actually help our family and heal our family.

Fathers HELP
A good father will always desire what is best for his family. The old saying, "I want my kids to have more than I did." proves that most fathers care about helping their kids do more, have more, be better, and accomplish greater things than they did. If you feel this way then congratulate yourself on desiring to be a good dad!

However, having these feelings and actually acting upon them are two different things. Sometimes we communicate these feelings with words, yet our actions teach something opposite. Let me explain. There are fathers in the world today that live vicariously through their children. The dad may have been a football star in high school so he may expect his son to also rise to the forefront of the sport.

I talked with a father once that said, "Every dad desires his son to be the star player on the team." I sat and listened, while thinking about his son. I knew his son had no desire to play sports, but was more interested in participating in arts and music. I stopped the dad in mid-thought and said, "Listen, not every dad has these desires for their kid to be the star player on the sports team. You need to stop living vicariously through your son and start helping him discover how God has wired him, not how God has wired you." He looked at me as if he never thought of parenting in that way.

The truth is, some dads desire their kid to be the star of the drama department or the head of the debate team. Each dad is different. Why? Because God wires each of us in uniquely different ways.

God gives each of us various gifts and talents, and He expects us to use them for His glory. This is also true of our family members. God has uniquely crafted them as well. It is not our job to dictate what they should become. It is our job to help them discover how God has designed them to be. We are called to HELP.

Most dads genuinely desire to help, but without even knowing it, many fathers actually hinder. If we were honest, we struggle with a bit of insecurity that leads us to put unnecessary pressure on our wife and kids to get them to perform. We do this because we want others outside of our family to think of us as a successful father. But, if those inside our family resent us, then who cares what anyone outside our family thinks?

Social media hinders this task as well. We only see the filtered version of every other family and we tend to compare that to the unfiltered, raw, and wrinkled version of our family. This comparison is never fair or accurate, and our family will always lose the comparison. The standard by which we live is not measured by other people, but by God's standard. Stop comparing your life and family to others and start looking to Jesus. Become the leader of your family that helps move your family closer to Jesus. Let Jesus worry about the fruit. You and I, as fathers, should focus on staying connected to the root. The fruit will come, but it may look different than we initially thought.

Fathers HEAL
Another thing fathers should do is HEAL. Healing is so important when it comes to building trust and security in the home. Becoming a source of healing to our family with our words and actions will produce more dividends than almost any other thing we do. Unfortunately, if we fail to heal our family, our behavior has the opposite effect. But, what is the opposite of heal? Harm. You might be thinking, "Hold on! I have never laid a hand on my wife or my children. I am not an abusive father." Well, that's good, but sometimes it is what we don't do that brings the most harm. Let me explain.

I have met so many men that grew up with a dad physically present in the home, but mentally he was elsewhere. The dad never laid a hand on the kids in an abusive way; but, he also never put a hand on them in any loving way either. This is just as harmful. In other situations, dads would never be physically abusive, but harsh and toxic words would run freely out of their mouth toward their wife and kids. This is just as harmful.

Wounds and scars are not always visible on the outside. Mental, emotional, and spiritual wounds on the inside are harder to see and more difficult to heal. If we are going to be good fathers, we must be intentional about the words and actions that bring healing to our family and not become the source of harm.

I know you desire to be a healing provider, but I also know that many dads have never thought they could be damaging their family or causing harm in this way. Financially providing for your family is an honorable thing to do; however, it is not the only thing to do. Let's be sure we are not unintentionally being a source of harm by mentally or emotionally checking out, or by using inappropriate language in our interactions with our wife and kids. Fathers HEAL.

Perhaps today you realize that you have unintentionally been a source of harm to your family and you desire to change this. The first step is to recognize the truth. The second step is to confess the truth. Talk to God about the issue and ask Him for forgiveness. He is faithful and just to forgive you (1 John 1:9). Next, ask Him to give you the wisdom to know how to make things right between you and your family. God gives wisdom freely to all who ask (James 1:5). Finally, go to your family and explain how God has been growing your wisdom and you realize you have unintentionally caused the family harm. Confess authentically and ask for forgiveness.

In many cases this will be enough to bring healing to the situation. However, there may be a need to talk with a pastor or counselor to help the family move towards reconciliation. Whatever it takes, be the source of healing in your family.

Fathers HELP and HEAL.

Bible Study Option

1. Read and discuss: Luke 10:25–37
2. What is the main point of this passage?
3. How did the Samaritan help and heal the victim?
4. What did the religious leaders do?
5. Have you been a good Samaritan to your family lately? To your church?
6. What will you do this week to live out and teach this principle to your family?
7. Can I hold you accountable to do this?

WHAT A FATHER DOES

CHAPTER 6:
ENCOURAGE AND EQUIP

Rewriting
FATHERS

Chapter 6: Fathers Encourage and Equip

The fifth letter in the acronym also stands for two words: ENCOURAGE and EQUIP. Let's spend a few moments talking about each word and discuss a few examples of what it looks like to actually encourage our family and equip our family.

Fathers Encourage
A good father will always desire to encourage his family with his words and with his presence. He will speak words of life and hope. With these words alone he will leave a positive legacy. A legacy forms when we do something so significant that it actually affects the generations that follow. A legacy never happens by accident; it is the result of intentional living. We build them when we live a life of selflessness, by focusing on others more than ourselves. The only way to affect the generations after us is to live forward; to live with eyes toward the future. We should live in the future. What encouragement can we provide now and in the coming years to help that bright future come true? We should train ourselves to see the future potential of every family member now.

One of the main reasons Jesus came to this earth was to restore the broken relationship that humans had with God. He was looking into the future, and He saw not what was, but what could be. Jesus knew that sin had broken God's perfect creation and He wanted to help broken people become whole. How would He do this? By becoming broken Himself. He would sacrifice His life on a Roman cross and rise from the dead on the third day, according to the scriptures.

Fifty days after His resurrection, He would pour out the Holy Spirit on one hundred and twenty people in an upper room and give them the same purpose: help broken people become whole. Jesus knew that when a broken person became whole, they would be so grateful and delighted that they would also want to pay it forward and help others heal, too. So, the cycle began in the first century and has continued until this day. As fathers, we are called to lead our kids and our spouse towards wholeness in Christ.

How do we do this? We must see the future person rather than the present person. We must not see what is, but what could be. As fathers, we need to encourage our kids and spouse to see the future possibility rather than just the present reality. If we are going to lead like Jesus, we must discipline ourselves to see with His eyes. How does Jesus see us? He sees the future. So should we. Consider speaking prophetically to your wife and children this week. Communicate what you see when you look at your son or daughter and what you believe God is gifting them to be in the future. This is not us mandating their future. It is us helping them imagine bigger aspirations for their future, pushing them beyond even their wildest dreams.

My dad spoke into me more than I saw was possible. His vision of my future helped me become a dreamer who never put limits on God's ability to do something. Hope is the goal of encouragement. Help your kids and wife dream of a better tomorrow, today.

Fathers Equip

Another thing fathers should do is EQUIP. Equipping means we provide the the items necessary to help others succeed in life. This principle is depicted in Philippians 2:4, which says, "Let each of you look not only to his own interests, but also to the interests of others."

A good father is considerate of the needs of his kids and spouse by providing the tools necessary for them to accomplish their tasks. As much as possible, we should provide opportunities and resources to help our family do what they need to do and also to help them reach their future goals and dreams. This could include offering the appropriate tools necessary for basic house chores and school supplies. It also means providing our family with training opportunities, equipment, or other assistance to help them become the best they can be at a hobby or future endeavor.

My parents noticed that I was showing interest in playing the guitar, so they eventually bought me a guitar and a few training books. They would later help me take guitar lessons and they gave me opportunities to play in front of people. Then, when I needed more equipment, they did the best they could to provide it for me. This is not spoiling a kid; it is equipping a son. There is a fine line between spoiling and equipping. Each father has to define that line for himself. A good indicator of our children becoming spoiled can be evident when the child begins to feel entitled to the resources, instead of feeling grateful to receive the gifts.

Equipping our family is a decision to help them become the best possible person they can be. I know every good father wants to provide everything their family needs to succeed. However, what happens when we can't afford something? We should do the best we can with what we have and not be afraid to ask for assistance from a close friend. Equipping the family sometimes means stepping out of the way for our family to be helped by someone else. Don't let pride get in the way of equipping your family.

Fathers ENCOURAGE and EQUIP.

Bible Study Option

1. Read and discuss the following verses: Ephesians 4:29, Colossians 4:6, Proverbs 18:20-21, and Proverbs 16:23-24
2. How have you been speaking to your family lately? To your church?
3. Have your words been a source of life or death?
4. Read and discuss: Philippians 2:3-8
5. How does this passage say our attitude should be to others, including our family?
6. What will you do this week to live out and teach this principle to your family?
7. Can I hold you accountable to do this?

"...encourage one another and build one another up..."

-1 Thessalonians 5:11

WHAT A FATHER DOES

CHAPTER 7:
RAISE AND REDIRECT

Rewriting
FATHERS

Chapter 7: Fathers Raise and Redirect

The sixth letter in the acronym also stands for two words: RAISE and REDIRECT. Let's spend a few moments talking about each word and discuss a few examples of what it looks like to actually raise our family and redirect our family.

Fathers Raise

A good father will always desire to raise his family towards a direction of health and maturity. Let's talk about what the word "raise" actually means. It refers to the act of bringing into being, or to bring up. This applies to a parent/child relationship. The term "child-rearing" is meant to convey bringing up a child in such a way as to direct them towards health and maturity. In the same way, good fathers will raise their family towards God and towards becoming better as human beings. This concept is connected to the previous chapter in that we, as fathers, should not look at what *is*, but what *could be* in the life of our family.

In this way, raising our family is another way to say "directing" our family. This does not mean we micromanage them, or lead in a dictatorial way. It means we lead the family. Good fathers read leadership books to help become better leaders, not just in his career but, more importantly, in his family. Good leaders don't push their followers from the back; they lead their followers from the front. The same is true of good fathers.

A father is like a quarterback. He is not the only player on the team, and he is dependent on all the other players. But he is the director of the team, and he has to make hard and fast decisions to the best of his ability to progress down the field. He gets his cues from a higher authority (the coach), but he is the one in the game directing the team towards victory. Fathers are the same way. We get our cues from a higher authority (Jesus), but we must lead and direct our family to move down the field and progress towards victory. This is what it means to raise our family well.

Fathers Redirect

A good father will also redirect his family at times. Going back to the analogy of the quarterback; there are times when he must call an audible to the play because of what he senses from the opposing team. In life, the opposing team is the enemy bent on destroying the marriage and the family unit. Good fathers are like good quarterbacks in that we can sense when a blitz is coming. It is during these times when we must be willing to redirect our family to protect them as well as help them continue to move forward. It is also during these times that we must be willing to take the hit when necessary and not divert from our responsibilities as the leader.

Another important principle in leading well is that sometimes moving forward means slowing down. Men tend to want to experience quick progress, so slowing down seems counterintuitive. But, if we move too fast, we might leave someone important behind.

Many years ago, I led a team of students on a mission trip to Seattle, WA. We had several vans, each with one adult driver and five or six teenagers. On one particular day, I put one of my volunteers in charge of leading the caravan to a specific location. As we were following behind him, I began to notice that he was going a few miles over the speed limit and was always trying to beat the red lights at intersections. Because of this, he was unintentionally leaving us behind as we got stuck at the red light. I called him and said, "Hey man, you are supposed to be leading us, not racing us." As soon as I voiced those words God spoke to me at that red light. He said, *"Preston, this is how you sometimes lead, too."*

I had to take a step back and repent because God was right. If I'm not careful, I will lead with such fury that I will unintentionally leave people behind. If we lead so fast that nobody can keep up with us, then are we really leading? In other words, if we look back and find nobody behind us, then we aren't leading at all. It is important to slow down at times to help the entire family stay together.

Sometimes we need to redirect our life as well. To direct and redirect our family, we must know where we are going and allow God to direct and redirect us. We will never be able to lead our family where we haven't gone ourselves. Are you allowing Jesus to direct your life? Are you open to the redirections God might ask of you from time-to-time? How flexible are you in letting the Holy Spirit redirect you from the path you are on now? If we, as fathers, are not easily redirected then our family won't be either. The family will take cues from us. When they see us submit to Jesus and allow Him to direct and redirect our life, they will begin to trust us enough to raise and redirect their life.

Consistency is another important principle in raising and redirecting our family. We must be steady and stable in our leadership and not be apathetic or off-the-cuff in our decision-making. We must take the position of father seriously and strive to make the best possible decisions for the health and well being of our family. Anger and quick-tempered outbursts are a sure way to diminish trust and loyalty when it comes to helping our family follow us well. John C. Maxwell is famous for saying, "Everything rises and falls on leadership." I know there are always exceptions to this rule; but, when our family struggles to follow us, chances are we need to redirect our style of leadership and use a different tactic. It is our job to raise and redirect our family toward God and health. Let's take that job more seriously than we do our career. Nothing is more important than leading our family well.

Fathers RAISE and REDIRECT.

Bible Study Option

1. Read and discuss: Deuteronomy 6:1-9
2. What does this passage teach us about our role as fathers?
3. What suggestions does it give us to teach our children the ways of God?
4. Are these suggestions still applicable today?
5. What are some ways you will begin to practice this principle in your home this week?
6. Can I hold you accountable with that?

Prepare the child for the road, not the road for the child.

WHAT A FATHER DOES

CHAPTER 8:
SERVE AND SHARE

Rewriting
FATHERS

Chapter 8: Fathers Serve and Share

The seventh letter in the acronym also stands for two words: SERVES and SHARES. Let's spend a few moments talking about each word and discuss a few examples of what it looks like to actually serve our family and share with our family.

Fathers Serve
A good father will always desire to serve his family's needs more than his own. Several years ago, I discovered that an idol is more than just a wood or stone statue. An idol is anything we value more than we value God.

I found that one of my idols is progress. I genuinely love people, but, if I am honest, I would have to admit that I often love progress more than people. There was a time when several of our team members at my church were mourning the loss of a few friends that decided to leave our church for another church. We all knew why they left and that we shouldn't change the identity of what God had called our church to be to keep them. But it didn't diminish the pain some members felt from the loss of close friends and committed volunteers.

All this time, I had been encouraging the team to shake it off and keep going. Tension began to grow between members of the team until it finally came to a head. I remember sitting in a reconciliation meeting and hearing them realize for the first time that they were slowing down progress in our team because they hadn't taken the time to mourn the loss of their friends effectively. In the same way, I finally understood that they were truly suffering, and because I had valued progress over people, I hadn't even thought about the fact that they were struggling like this. I was not serving them well. I openly said I was sorry for loving progress more than them and that I desired to make things right between us. After this incident, we all had a healthier view of what it means to put others ahead of yourself, and we all began to serve one another better.

The incident at the reconciliation meeting also shifted my personal views in other areas of my life. I even began to look at my family differently. I am constantly fighting against the idol of progress and am learning to value people more. Our family is the most important thing in our lives, and we must protect them from our insecurities or desires. Much harm has been done in the name of progress. Families have been torn apart in pursuit of happiness and success.

Jesus tells us to love our neighbor as ourselves. Our family is included in the word "neighbor." Think of it this way: Would you want your wife to forget dates that are important to you? Would you want your kids to miss important events at your work that you value? Do you want your family to dismiss your words because they don't think your feelings are valid? If we are not careful, we will begin to serve our desires and our version of what a family should be instead of actually serving the true version that our family really is. Don't serve a "dream version" when you have the real version sitting right in front of you. Serving your family doesn't mean thinking less of yourself; it means thinking of yourself less.

Fathers Share
A good father will always desire to share with his family. I know this should go without saying, but it is a good reminder for us, as dads, to never have an attitude of "this is mine, and that is yours." A healthy father understands that everything he has should be available to his wife and children. Obviously, there are things that we should keep out of reach of children, like medicines or our credit card information. This doesn't mean we shouldn't give them what they need out of our supplies when the occasion arises. We are called to be wise and to be good managers of our "things," but we are also called to be benevolent with all that we have in order to care for the needs of others.

Jesus uses an illustration of an earthly father to convey a truth about the Heavenly Father when he says, *"Or which one of you, if his son asks him for bread, will give him a stone? Or if he asks for a fish, will give him a serpent? If you then, who are evil, know how to give good gifts to your children, how much more will your Father who is in heaven give good things to those who ask him!"* (Matthew 7:9-11)

When Jesus uses the word "evil," he does not mean that we are demonic. He is saying that we are sinful and imperfect. Yet, even in this blemished condition, we genuinely desire to give our kids what they need and ask for. How much more does our perfect Heavenly Father desire to give His children what we need and ask for? We are called to be like our Heavenly Father as much as humanly possible. We will be a picture to our children of what God is like, so let's take this calling of fatherhood seriously!

We should share what we have to meet the needs and desires of our family. This may mean we don't have two separate checking accounts. It may mean we share passwords to our computer and phone with our spouse. I personally never want my wife to think I am hiding anything or keeping anything from her. We are always open and honest with every area of our lives because this is what it means to share.

Sharing also means more than just making our monetary items accessible to our family. It may mean giving our influence and opportunities away as well. I remember having a friend who was given great opportunities in life, not just because he was talented, but also because of who his father was. His dad was an influential person and was able to share his influence with his son in order to open up doors for him that otherwise may have been closed. I remember thinking, "I want to be that type of dad. I want my children to not only have 'things' I never had. I also want them to have 'opportunities' I never had." I decided to work hard at developing an influence with people so that one day I could share that influence with my sons.

Do you have an influential position in your career? Are you well known? What do you have, as far as opportunities, that you have been holding onto and perhaps you need to begin to share with your family?

Finally, sharing is more than monetary things or opportunity and influence. Sharing is also opening up our hearts to our family. A good father will let his kids and wife see inside his mind and feelings. Many men are a closed book to their family members. For some reason, we think men shouldn't cry, share deep thoughts, or confess when we have made mistakes, as if in some way that would be revealing our weaknesses and we might be viewed as a failure in the eyes of our family.

Nothing could be further from the truth. Think about it. There is something compelling about a man tearing up over something he is passionate about. It moves the room. Men don't usually do that, so when it happens, everybody knows it is time to pay attention. Don't be afraid to shed a tear in front of your wife and children when you are emotionally moved by them or by God. This is a healthy thing for kids to see.

I want my children to know I love them and that they tap into my emotional soul. I want my wife to see me weep over her when we share deep things of the heart. I want my family to see me become passionately stirred when I encounter Jesus through worship. I want to be an open book to my family, so they know I am human and that they are allowed to be human as well.

I also want to write and document my thoughts, experiences, struggles, passions, ambitions, dreams, etc. I want my family to find these writings when I pass so they can get a glimpse into the heart of a father and know that I have always loved them. I want them to pass these writings down to their children and grandchildren. I want to leave a positive legacy.

I believe it is the desire of every father, and every man, to leave a lasting legacy that lives beyond their life. If this is the case with you, then take the Legacy Journal in this book seriously. Consider ways to share your journal with your children at certain milestones in their life, like becoming a teenager, getting their Driver's License, or High School graduation. There are prompts to help you journal strategically. Use the F.A.T.H.E.R.S. acronym as a way to teach your son what a father IS and what a father DOES. Use it for your daughter to help her know what type of man she should one day marry. Share one of these journals with your friends and family members. Start a fathers accountability group, or small group, with the purpose of holding each other accountable to live up to this "job description" of what a father IS and what a father DOES.

However you decide to continue in this journey, I want to thank you for committing your time to read this book and participating in the legacy journal. By investing your time in this way, you are on the right path towards leaving a positive legacy to your family.

In closing, Ben Franklin is credited as saying, *"If you want to be remembered when you are dead, then do something worth writing or write something worth reading."* I don't know about you, but at the end of my life, I hope to have done both. I would like to finish this section by speaking over you the same blessing I recite over my kids often. This blessing is a modified version of Numbers 6:24-26.

"May the Lord bless you and keep you.

May His face shine upon you and be gracious to you.

May He turn His face towards you and give you peace.

In the name of the Father, the Son, and the Holy Spirit. Amen!"

It is my prayer that more dads would speak blessings like this over their children, that they would lead their families to the throne of Grace, and that they would take seriously their call to rewriting what it means to be godly F.A.T.H.E.R.S.

Bible Study Option

1. Read and discuss: John 13:1-17
2. Why was it so significant for Jesus to be the one washing their feet?
3. In the world's eye should Jesus have been the one serving like this?
4. What other lies does the world teach about what leadership looks like?
5. Have you been leading your family the way Jesus led His disciples, or have you been leading the way the world tells us to lead?
6. What is one thing you will do this week to begin leading your family like Jesus?
7. How will you teach this principle to your kids this week?
8. Can I hold you accountable with that?

Great satisfaction comes from sharing with others.

CHAPTER 9:
THE LEGACY JOURNAL

Rewriting
FATHERS

Chapter 9: The Legacy Journal

Why should a father journal?
Well, let's start with the idea of a journal. What is it? Why should you do it? A journal is simply a collection of your own thoughts, your personal reflections, your own observations, your own meaning in life, your experiences, and your views on the world around you as you witness it daily, weekly, monthly, or yearly. It can help clear your mind, keep track of decisions, track progress, and remember or share who you are. However, it is the last one that is the primary reason why we created this particular book. We want dads to share who they really are with their kids.

But isn't this child's play? Isn't it for schoolgirls? There's often this idea of journaling being likened to a kid keeping a diary with the drama about friends or bullies or little love notes about that adorable girl or boy in math class...covered in doodles and sketch art. But, as we grow into adulthood, and more specifically in this case fatherhood, the idea of journaling takes on far more meaning with more power behind it.

Looking back, we can find records of many men who journaled; in fact, some very influential men. The list includes historical men like Albert Einstein, Mark Twain, Lewis and Clark, Thomas Edison, Leonardo da Vinci, Benjamin Franklin, President Ronald Reagan, Ernest Hemingway, Winston Churchill, and George S Patton. But, it also includes more recent celebrities like Bruce Lee, George Lucas, and Tim Ferriss. Even King David of the Bible is known to write down his thoughts and feelings in the book of Psalms.

All of these men wrote for different reasons; but, at its foundation, their journal was whatever they made it to be. Your's can be whatever you make it to be, too. It is all you. Write to pass it down. Or, just write for your own style of therapy or productivity.

How does this work?
We wanted to take a section of this book and discuss why journaling is important, especially as a dad aspiring to simply be better and to leave a legacy behind for his family. We hope that this can possibly even inspire you to take it further than this book. At the minimum, use the prompts on each writing page and complete this book. For yourself or for your children; hopefully both.

Maybe you keep the book to yourself, tucked away somewhere private. But, our prayer is that you make an intentional plan to pass it on to your child or children at a certain age or milestone later in life, such as turning a certain age or when they graduate high school or college. Perhaps when they get married, or maybe when they find out they will become a Dad; whatever milestone you may decide. You get the point. If you do that, remember it as you write; with purpose. Each word, phrase, or sentence may be something they hold onto as precious in their life. They will keep this book as a forever legacy of you that they return to in times of reflection, introspection, or just when they need a reminder of you.

Why is this such a big deal to us?
Going back a couple of generations, our family recalls our grandfather being a proud WWII war veteran that merited two Purple Heart Medals; but, he kept those stories and lessons closely guarded. He rarely spoke of the war because it brought him pain and sorrow to think of the men who he fought shoulder to shoulder with in battle and how so many had given their lives in sacrifice. We wish we knew more. We wish someone had asked more questions. We wish that he would have been gifted a journal to let all of that out. It may have made him an even finer man and release himself of those struggles while showing us more about him.

Beyond the war, he matured into a quiet, strong, diligent, and faithful servant to Christ, our grandmother, and his four children. His youngest son, our father, was the same way....except for the quiet part. His laugh was contagious. His smile was warming, and his stories...they are legends still repeated today. So, our Dad's early passing at age 54 sent shockwaves through our entire family. He was a great man of a great many stories. He could recall a life lesson for almost any situation.

And he journaled; although for only a very short season in life. But to this day, we hold those writings, those porthole windows into his life, as something more valuable than any possession he owned or passed on to us. We could see that he wanted to record his life. He wanted to jot down his feelings, his emotions, his faith, and his observations. It was surely therapeutic for him. It has definitely been that for us. It was an opportunity to know him like never before. It helped us see a different side of our father and understand him on a deeper level.

Anyone that knew our Dad closely at all has undoubtedly, at some point, wished that they could just sit down with him, his magnetic persona, and a cup of coffee to experience, once more, any story he wanted to tell. It would be a blessing to hear one more time the riveting tales about his life growing up with his twin sister Betty in a rural setting; or the wild-spirited adventures of his youth; or his maturing, persistent pursuit of Christ; or of any of the other interesting things he saw (and did) during his life that was cut too short on Earth.

We wish everyone could be so blessed to have a Dad like ours. He shared all kinds of memories with us as we grew up, even if only briefly. But, maybe you grew up with an absent father in whatever way; physically perhaps, or even just emotionally. We've seen the pain of absent fathers. We hope you can break that cycle in your family history. Or, maybe your father is still alive, present or not in your life, and you want to know more about him. Give him this book. Ask him to complete it. Maybe, you could even do it as a project for each of you together.

Why & how do you tell your own story?
For us, in our own lives as fathers now, we deeply feel the responsibility to our children and their children to share our faith, our struggles, our funny stories, our fears, and just simply ourselves. We want them to know us, and we want them to pass on our stories, our faith, and our lessons in hopes that their generation will somehow be bettered by it. Maybe they would understand more of the process behind decisions we made, paths we chose, and how we feel they formed who we are today and the generations to follow.

We believe many other men & fathers want to do this. But where do they start? How do you tell the story of your life? How do you share your own life lessons? It's easier to record this than you think. It doesn't have to be an epic autobiography. A few sentences written down a day or even a week in a journal can be telling enough. It doesn't have to be eloquent. You'll get better the more you write. Your ability to write is far less important than your commitment to it.

We knew many men would need help getting started. So, we provided some prompts; some starter thoughts, to help you along the way. This book is intended to provide a route to writing that will challenge and improve your own life as a father along the path. Do a page a day. Or a few pages in a day. Or only a page every week. Let it take 3 months or a year to complete. But, make a goal to finish it. Set a schedule. Maybe even set a reminder for yourself somewhere so that you remember. Or leave it at your bedside so you see it each evening.

Our prayer for you and all fathers is to adapt and apply the lessons in this book, but to also use this as a tool to help pass down a little more of you to your children. Hopefully, one day they will understand more about you and be able to take that small window of lessons from your life and improve on them to better their family and their own lives.

Whatever it takes, make it important. Make it something you "get to do" not "have to do." Smile when you do it. Remember who you are. And please, share it with the next generation.

this journal belongs to:

_____

Given by:

_____

To be passed on to:

_____

I AM THANKFUL TO BE/BECOME A DAD BECAUSE:

LAY YOUR HAND ON THIS PAGE AND TRACE AROUND IT:

AS A DAD, I AM ENJOYING OR LOOKING FORWARD TO:

SHARE ABOUT YOUR FIRST CAR. WHAT WAS IT? WHERE DID YOU GET IT? HOW LONG DID YOU HAVE IT? WHERE WAS YOUR FIRST BIG DRIVE?

HOW DO YOU REACT WHEN YOU THINK OF YOUR FATHER? IS THERE JOY? SADNESS? PRIDE? ANGER?

WHAT IS SOMETHING UNIQUE ABOUT YOUR HOMETOWN? WHAT WOULD YOU WANT TO BE REMEMBERED ABOUT YOUR HOMETOWN?

SOME GOALS I HAVE FOR MY CHILD/CHILDREN ARE:

SHARE A RANDOM MEMORY BY DRAWING IT IN COMIC BOXES:

WHAT WAS YOUR MOM LIKE — PHYSICALLY, MENTALLY, EMOTIONALLY? WHAT WAS LIFE LIKE WITH HER?

WHAT PET(S) DID YOU HAVE GROWING UP? WHAT WERE THEIR NAMES, AND WHAT DID YOU DO TOGETHER?

DRAW A PICTURE OF YOUR FAVORITE MEAL:

ONE VALUABLE LESSON ABOUT LIFE I WOULD LIKE TO TEACH MY KIDS IS:

DESCRIBE YOUR CHILDHOOD HOME(S). WHERE DID YOU LIVE? WHAT DID YOU LIKE ABOUT IT? OR DID YOU MOVE AROUND A LOT? STAY IN ONE PLACE?

WHO HAS BEEN A SIGNIFICANT INFLUENCE IN YOUR LIFE (LIKE A MENTOR)? WAS IT A SPECIFIC FRIEND OR A PASTOR OR SOMEONE ELSE? WHO SPOKE INTO YOUR LIFE AND HELPED MOLD YOU INTO WHO YOU ARE TODAY?

THE BEST ADVICE I WAS EVER GIVEN WAS:

MY FAVORITE PART OF BEING AN ADULT IS:

WHAT HOBBIES DID YOU HAVE GROWING UP? HOW DID THEY SHAPE WHO YOU ARE TODAY?

ONE VALUABLE LESSON ABOUT WORK I WOULD LIKE TO TEACH MY KIDS IS:

_____
_____
_____
_____
_____
_____
_____
_____
_____
_____
_____
_____
_____
_____
_____
_____
_____
_____
_____
_____
_____
_____

IF I WERE GRANTED THREE WISHES, I WOULD WISH FOR:

WHAT WAS YOUR FAVORITE BIRTHDAY AS A CHILD? WHAT WERE YOUR AVERAGE PARTIES LIKE?

WHAT DID YOUR ROOM LOOK LIKE AS A CHILD? HOW WAS IT DECORATED? WAS IT SHARED WITH A SIBLING?

MY RELATIONSHIP WITH JESUS BEGAN:

WHAT WAS IT LIKE FINDING OUT YOU WERE GOING TO HAVE A CHILD? WERE YOU SURPRISED OR WAS IT PLANNED?

MY FAVORITE BIBLE VERSE, PASSAGE, OR STORY IS:

SHARE A RANDOM MEMORY BY DRAWING IT IN COMIC BOXES:

WHAT MUSIC DID YOU LISTEN TO GROWING UP? WHAT MUSIC DID YOUR PARENTS OR SIBLINGS LISTEN TO? DID THEY LIKE YOUR MUSIC?

WHEN THEY GET OLDER, I HOPE MY KIDS ENJOY:

IF I COULD LIVE ANYWHERE IN THE WORLD, MY LIFE WOULD LOOK LIKE:

ONE VALUABLE LESSON I WOULD LIKE TO TEACH MY KIDS ABOUT MARRIAGE IS:

WHO WERE YOUR BEST FRIENDS IN ELEMENTARY SCHOOL? WHAT DID YOU LIKE ABOUT THEM? WHAT DID YOU DO TOGETHER?

I HOPE MY KIDS' MOTHER KNOWS:

AT MY BEST, I HOPE TO BE:

WHEN PEOPLE SPEAK OF ME, I HOPE THEY SAY AND FEEL:

DRAW OUT A STORY OF WHEN YOU ACTED LIKE A DAREDEVIL USING COMIC BOOK BOXES:

HAVE YOU EVER PLAYED ANY SPORTS? WHAT HAVE YOU LEARNED THROUGH SPORTS?

ONE VALUABLE LESSON I WOULD LIKE TO TEACH MY KIDS ABOUT FAITH IS:

ONE IMPORTANT LESSON I WOULD LIKE TO TEACH MY KIDS ABOUT FAMILY IS:

WHAT FAMILY TRADITIONS DID YOU HAVE GROWING UP? DID THEY REVOLVE AROUND HOLIDAYS? MEALS? WEEKENDS? A CERTAIN SEASON?

WHAT MOVIE HAVE YOU SEEN THAT REALLY MOVED YOU? WHY? WHAT WAS THE STORY IN IT?

I HOPE MY FAMILY KNOWS:

THE GREAT EXCHANGE

The Great Exchange is the story of what Jesus did for us when He died on a cross 2,000 years ago. There are four words we will look at in this story: Fall, Left, Jesus, Right.

FALL

The word "fall" represents all of humanity. Before we start a relationship with Jesus we are in a fallen condition and we will have no peace and no joy. There is a verse in the Bible that says, "For all have sinned and FALLEN short of the glory of God." (Romans 3:23) Picture an archer aiming at a target and the arrow falling short of the bulls-eye. No matter how good we might be, we have all fallen short of God's perfection. This is called sin and this verse teaches that everybody is in this condition. We have all fallen short of God's perfection.

LEFT

The next word is "left". If we are LEFT in this fallen condition we will continue to experience a lack of love, acceptance, peace, and joy. We will continue to feel insecure and worthless. The Bible shares a verse that says, "The wages (or what we earn) of sin is death..." In other words, if we are left in this fallen condition we will not only experience a physical death one day, but we will also experience a spiritual death, known as Hell, for eternity. We will be separated from God after we die. This is the bad news. But what can we do? Well, the rest of that verse actually says, "But the gift of God is eternal life through Jesus Christ our Lord!" (Romans 6:23)

JESUS

The third word is "Jesus". We learn in this verse that what Jesus did for us on the cross was powerful enough to take away our sins and remove us from this fallen condition. In fact, another verse in the Bible says it this way: "God made Him who knew no sin to be sin on our behalf so that we might become the righteousness of God." (2 Corinthians 5:21)

This is called the "Great Exchange". Jesus lived a perfect, sinless life. Yet he exchanged his perfection for our imperfections. He exchanged his righteousness for our sinfulness by dying on the cross.

RIGHT

If we will just accept his payment for sin on the cross and apply it to our lives then we will no longer be LEFT in a fallen condition but will be made RIGHT with God. We can actually become the righteousness of God. Fall. Left. Jesus. Right. This is called the "Great Exchange" and it is definitely GOOD NEWS! This is the Gospel. Will you accept it today?

If you have never confessed your sins to Jesus and have never asked Him to forgive you then you can do that right now. All you need to do is acknowledge your need for Him to exchange His perfection for your imperfection and ask Him to make you a new person. Start a relationship with Jesus and make Him the Lord of your life. Consider praying to Him right now this simple prayer:

"Dear Jesus, I recognize I have fallen short of your perfection and I need you to exchange your perfection for my imperfection. I commit my life to you and will no longer live for myself, but will let you be my king. I give my life to you and ask you to save me and make me a new person. I confess my sins and ask for forgiveness. I will live for you for the rest of my life. In Jesus' name, amen!"

If you just prayed this prayer then congratulations! You have just started a relationship with Jesus! You are forgiven of your sins and are now part of the family of God. We encourage you to tell your pastor and church about this decision. If you don't have a pastor or a church we encourage you to go online and look for a Christian church near you in order to get involved as soon as possible. It is important for you to talk to a spiritual leader and get mentored by them so you will better understand what it means to follow Jesus. We are so proud of you! We also highly encourage you to tell your family what just happened. As the leader of your family you should encourage them to become a follower of Jesus too!

For more information on what it means to be a Christian, and to learn more about the Bible, visit www.rewritingfathers.com/bible

TEACHING THESE PRINCIPLES TO KIDS

How to teach the F.A.T. principles to our children

There are certain principles in this book that our children need to learn. Use the following question/answer format to train a child in the way they should go. Simply choose one of the questions listed below and spend an entire week helping your child learn the answer from memory.

Be patient with them. Use this method of learning as you tuck your child into bed at night. On the first night ask them a question and then teach them the answer. On the second night ask them the same question and encourage them to recite as much of the answer as they can from memory. Correct them when they get it wrong. Repeat this every night until they have successfully recited the answer from memory two nights in a row. Then move to the next question on the list below.

Questions and Answers

Question: Who is God?
Answer: God is the creator of the universe and everything in it.

Question: How many Gods are there?
Answer: There is only one God.

Question: As a family member, what are we are called to be?
Answer: As a family member, we are called to be faithful, available, and teachable to God, our family, our church, and our work/school.

Question: Who is Jesus?
Answer: Jesus is God in flesh. He died for our sins and made forgiveness available to us. He is our Lord and Savior.

Question: What is the Gospel?
Answer: The Gospel is the story of Jesus' life, death, burial, and resurrection for our sins.

Question: What is sin?
Answer: Sin is doing, thinking, or saying anything that falls short of God's perfection.

Question: How do we become a Christian?
Answer: We become a Christian when we admit we have sinned, believe Jesus died and rose again for our sin, and confess our sin to Jesus. We must ask for forgiveness and give our life to Jesus.

Question: Who is the Holy Spirit?
Answer: The Holy Spirit is God in spirit. He lives in us and leads us to know truth. He gives us spiritual gifts to use in the church.

Question: Why should we be faithful, available, and teachable to God?
Answer: We should be faithful, available, and teachable to God because He created us, died for us, and lives in us as Christians. He is our Lord and Savior.

Question: What is the family?
Answer: The family is God's first institution and begins when a man and a woman enter into a covenant relationship called marriage.

Question: Why should we be faithful, available, and teachable to our family?
Answer: We should be faithful, available, and teachable to our family because God commanded it and the family is an earthly picture of God's relationship with humanity.

Question: What is the church?
Answer: The church is God's second institution. It is not a building. It is the body and the bride of Christ. It is the collection of all Christians everywhere.

Question: Why should we be faithful, available, and teachable to the church?
Answer: We should be faithful, available, and teachable to the church because God commanded it and it is Jesus' bride. We must treat the bride of Christ as good as we treat our mother.

Question: What is our work/school?
Answer: Our work/school is an opportunity to worship God through excellence. It is a blessing, not a burden.

Question: Why should we be faithful, available, and teachable in our work/school?
Answer: We should be faithful, available, and teachable in our work/school because God commanded it and it is a privilege to work and learn.

Question: What is the order of priorities in life?
Answer: God, Family, Church, Work

TEACHING THESE PRINCIPLES TO KIDS

Teaching the H.E.R.S. principles to our children

When you teach the following principles to your son begin by saying, "Son, one day you will be a husband, and possibly a father. You need to know what a father does and what type of woman you should one day marry."

When you teach the following principles to your daughter begin by saying, "One day you will be a wife and possibly a mother. You need to know what a wife does and what type of man you should one day marry."

Question: What do parents do for their family?
Answer: Parents help and heal, encourage and equip, raise and redirect, and they serve and share.

Question: What is the opposite of help and heal?
Answer: The opposite of help is hinder. The opposite of heal is harm. We should never hinder and harm anyone because they are made in the image of God.

Question: How can we encourage our family?
Answer: We can encourage our family by using positive words at all times. We should never speak negatively about those we love.

Question: How can we equip our family?
Answer: We can equip our family by giving of our time, energy, money, and resources to help them reach their goals and dreams.

Question: What does it mean to raise the family?
Answer: To raise the family means to lead the family towards health and towards Jesus.

Question: Who is supposed to raise the family?
Answer: The parents are supposed to raise the family. The children are supposed to follow the God-given leadership of mom and dad as long as they lead the family towards health and towards Jesus.

Question: What does it mean to redirect the family?

Answer: Redirecting the family means mom and dad makes appropriate changes at appropriate times for the sake of protecting us from harm and continuing to lead us towards health and towards Jesus.

Question: What does it mean to serve the family?

Answer: Serving the family means thinking less about your own desires and needs, and thinking more about the desires and needs of the other family members.

Question: What does it mean to share with the family?

Answer: Sharing with the family means giving access to what we have to family members in need. It also means we don't hold secrets about our life. We share openly about our thoughts, desires, and struggles.

Question: What are the only two institutions God established?

Answer: The only two institutions God established were the family and the church.

Question: How should we respond to these two institutions?

Answer: We should always prioritize, participate with, strengthen, honor, and protect both.

END NOTES

1 Mr Universe. Narrated by Jim Gaffigan. The Warner Theatre, Washington D.C., August 28, 2012.

2 The Father Effect: Positive Effects of Involved Dads." The Father Effect: Positive Effects of Involved Dads | Family Life. Accessed April 28, 2019. http://pathwaystofamilywellness.org/Family-Life/the-father-effect-positive-effects-of-involved-dads.html

3 Witt, Lance. High-impact Teams: Where Healthy Meets High Performance. Grand Rapids, MI: BakerBooks, a Division of Baker Publishing Group, 2018. Pg. 54

Made in the USA
Columbia, SC
25 May 2019